THE RIDE HOME

Ex Libris

THE RIDE HOME

Judith Hemschemeyer

October 17, 1987

To Lee,
who takes me in and makes
me feel at home,
love,
Judy

Texas Tech University Press
Lubbock, Texas, U.S.A.

1987

Acknowledgements

Permission from the following to reprint the poems listed is gratefully acknowledged.

Ark River Review: "Delos" (formerly "Mahler's Symphony # 2" and in a slightly different version)
Calyx: "The Monster's Flowered Apron," "O Mother My Giant Redwood"
Cincinnati Poetry Review: "February 11, 1963"
Green House: ". . .din"
Kansas Quarterly: "To My Next Poem"
Middle Jersey Writers, An Anthology of Poetry and Fiction: "My Mother Trying to Die"
National Forum: "Her Hands," "The Orphans' Harmonica Band"
Pavement: "It's When I Tried to Tame You," "News," "Recitative," "And Your Favorite Had Her Face Kissed Raw"
Plum: "Palabras Para Hoy"
Poetspeak: In Their Work, About Their Work: "First Love"
Portland Review: "Epithalamion," "I Dreamed That Dream"
Quarterly West: "The Back Hall Was All Wrong," "Evening and Mother and I"
Tangled Vines, A Collection of Mother and Daughter Poems: "The Petals of the Tulips"
The Hudson Review: "All These Things She Kept in Her Heart," "Obsession," "Icon," "Instead You Call" (formerly "Best Friends"), "Prayer After Mass," "Amimetobian," "Getting Ready to Translate Akhmatova," "Something Silver in the Air," "The Week You Were Dying," "Wedding Night," "The Method," "It's Dead," "To the Victor," "Chinese Baby," "Versailles"
The Iowa Review: "Indulgence and Accidents"
The Panhandler: "The Painters"
Three Rivers Poetry Journal: "Penelope"

The Ride Home, by Judith Hemschemeyer, is published in cooperation with the Associated Writing Programs as the 1986 winner of the Edith Shiffert Prize in Poetry in the AWP Award Series.

ISBN 0-89672-152-3 (paper)
ISBN 0-89672-153-1 (cloth)
Library of Congress Catalog Card Number: 87-50515
Designed by Lisa Goble, set in Baskerville,
    printed on White Hammermill Offset Opaque, 70 lb.
Texas Tech University Press, Lubbock, Texas 79409-1037
Copyright 1987 Texas Tech University Press
Printed in the United States of America

Foreword

When a grown daughter begins a search for her mother, she is bound to fear finding herself. Even if her memory serves the nostalgia of a happy childhood, happy among the playful rituals, games, toys and bedtime stories, it's bound to serve, among other things, to remind her those happy times are long since gone. The daughter laps her mother's age. She *sees* in the mirror; she hears, perhaps obscurely, her mother's voice in her own, too close to home; she recognizes a posture or gesture, a grin or grimace, as it fixes itself on her flesh forever.

There is a child's story about a young rabbit who yearns to set itself free from its mother's house. But the poor rabbit is doomed to failure. When the rabbit becomes a fish, a flower, or a bird, its mother becomes a fly fisherman, an English gardener, or the only tree in the neighborhood. Finally, in what must be an act of rabbit desperation, it becomes a human child, only to find itself running full steam ahead into its now human mother's open, and a little smug, arms as she stands on the threshhold of their modestly landscaped and neatly scrubbed middle-class cottage.

The first nineteen poems in Judith Hemschemeyer's *The Ride Home*, present, in bold strokes, in broad relief, the horrendous details of a daughter's literal and metaphorical ride home. Here the grown daughter's voice and memory serve the obsessions of her own unhappy childhood, a result of her mother's unhappy childhood, and the cause of her own children's pain in years to come. When the narrator says, "Maybe the ride home will never end," she means it.

In the course of one of the book's many rides the mother reaches out her long arms to wrench her family in her family's car off the road, while her vaguely present husband hums along at 80 miles per hour. Later, stopped in a motel, the daughter notices how her mother, now named Kali, Hindu destructive mother with her garland of skulls and belt of severed hands, pretends, as she hands out the family's socks, that she hasn't noticed she's just tried to kill them all. Paradox isn't always what it seems.

This mother goes at everything with an axe. She smashes her wedding ring, smashes one of her "dreamy" daughters in the face, bloodies the narrator/daughter's nose. Each thing she splits open reveals the possibility of more pain, it's all fuel for an already over-heated fire. And each thing she splits manages to fight back pitifully little; she's left with no more than a splinter, a small, persistent irritation, while those against whom she strikes out are left with huge and chronic obsessions.

When she isn't doing violence she is doing housework, cooking, cleaning, wallpapering the hall. Throughout these episodes the narrator/daughter is self-consciously aware of her mother's destructive powers. She is frightened and doomed. She tells her mother this; she says she's "frightened, Mother,/and I was you."

Even when the newly dead mother is on her own air freight ride to burial ("O Mother My Giant Redwood," p.21), the daughter dreams of and is a bit amused by her mother's rage at finding herself dead. Mother is not quite the spectre of the living dead. After all, this is a dream, but like the living dead of horror films who remind us how thin is the veneer of reason, the enraged, dead mother, not the fear-riddled and slightly giddy daughter, emerges as the force of will and action in the poem's conclusion. The daughter's dream transforms the dead into the living dead and the daughter's waking dream transforms her mother into a giant redwood. Like a child comforting herself in the face of recurrent terrors or monsters, the daughter/narrator speaks to her mother:

> O Mother my giant redwood.
>
> felled at last
> you let us live.
>
> You lay all morning quiet in the hold
>
> nimbus   black bloodclots
> dissolving   slowly letting go.

The rest of the book, in four more parts, by turns addresses loss of innocence in adolesence, early marriage, children and divorce, a painful love affair, and finally, somewhat retrospectively, the forces in the meditation of art the narrator believes may comfort her. Each section, however, recalls by mood, tone and result, how little the "slowly letting go" lets go.

What the narrator learns as a child from other children is the story of a paradise inhabited by worms, rats, and mice, of human desire so askew it longs for war to never end. From a neighbor she learns how to kill the newborn. From a friend, how children can take away the will to live. From her marriage she learns she can be as enraged as her mother. And she discovers her husband, in death, joins her mother among the dead who will not let go. From a lover she learns she still may play the role of obedient daughter. In "To the Victor," the narrator/daughter/lover learns her lover wants not only her but another woman as well. She's told, "Make her fall in love with you too," much in the way her mother sent her with dream money to the store to buy milk.

Only in the book's final section, when she calls upon the Bible, Muriel Rukeyser, Mandelstam, ancient mythology, Plutarch, Akhmatova and the Muse, does the narrator find some solace in mystery exceeding reason and the facts of her life. Here we find whom she wishes her ancestors to be; here she finds an aspect of herself more humorous, more daring, more courageous:

> Come closer if you want to know.
>
> But know too that when they asked me
> if there was anything I wouldn't write about
>
> I had to say no.

How broadly we interpret *anything* will determine how thoroughly these lines are to be believed. Judith Hemschemeyer's book is about pain, not about healing and forgiveness. With cool accuracy of isolated, unadorned detail, in deceptively curtailed rhythms, she writes a poetry of judgment and purification.

Dara Wier
Amherst
1987

Contents

III

IV

V

I

The Work of Her that went,
The Toil of Fellows done—
In Ovens green our Mother bakes,
By Fires of the Sun.

Emily Dickinson, Poem 1143

First Love

We fell in love at *Journey for Margaret*,
my mother and I. I was the same age
as Margaret O'Brien, braids and all

and she put her arm on the back of my chair
and touched my head and found the lump
I'd got that morning and forgot I had.

"What's this?" she whispered and I whispered back
I'd cracked my head against the brick wall
of the Savings and Loan walking backwards to school.

And the waves of her giggles washed over me
there in the dark. I had astonished her!
No telling what I'd do next!

But whatever it was, I knew that from then on
what happened between us was just as important
as Margaret O'Brien getting adopted up there on the screen.

Her Hands

were   "Big as a foot," she laughed.

When we walked downtown
one of her fingers was enough
for me to wrap my hand around.

Her hands
swooping for my forehead,
checking it for fever,
covered my whole face and I breathed bleach,
onions, beet juice, lemons, stew meat, wax,
whatever she'd been plunged in
when she turned to look at me.

Her hands
could hit, too,
could make my nose spurt blood
all down my blouse
that time I gave a snotty answer
before church.

I just stood there.

Then, after her third heart attack,
Dad pulled out some change to buy cigarettes
and showed me her wedding ring,
a lump of metal smashed beyond repair.

"She did it with the ax," he said.

As she did everything.

But no,

remember that Halloween
she hung apples in the kitchen on a string?
Hands behind our backs,
we tried and tried to take a bite.
Then she laughed and stepped in,
took a whole apple in her mouth
and said she'd won.

Her mouth
was lovely,
and so wide
that once on a dare from Dad
she opened it
and put the silver berry spoon inside.

With Only Dream Money

She lay on her back asleep,
her arms, her naked flesh and bones
above her head

and I,
tiny hyena,
crouched watching.

Then her mouth twitched
and she said, "Here's money.
Go to the store and get some milk."

And I knew I should
because she said I should.

But how could I go with only dream money?

And anyway she might talk again
while I was gone,

telling me to do
something I really could do
and had better do,

because what if she was just pretending?
What if she was watching too?

Anger Was Hers

Anger was hers
and beautiful skin
and long, strong hands

and so I had to pick my face
and curse beneath my breath
and bite my grubby nails to the quick,

make friends with Daddy, whistle,
learn to play dice,
throw like a boy,

lie:
when I wet my pants outdoors
I told her it was the wind that made them cold.

Anger was hers,
and the stove, the couch, the mirrors,
the walls because she kept them clean.

All I had was a jittery digestion
and my vomit
and with it

—like that ad for paint
that showed a globe of the world
dripping thick, viscous red—

night after night, week after week,
I was trying to *Cover the Earth*:
my sleeping sister and our bed.

Somewhere Near By

Every Monday she got up at dawn
to start the wash

and patrolled her garden,

bending to each flower,
barely touching it,

still in her bathrobe,
not dressed and angry yet,

her arms as strong as Joan of Arc's,
her hands that could reach everywhere

crossed on her chest
against the chill,

or brushing off a spiderweb
so the first slow bees would be safe.

No hives in our neighborhood,

so somewhere near by
there must have been a shed,

a whole barn full of honey.

The Painters

Everything was yellow:
the warm, milk-yellow paint
they got by mixing in the white
and stirring it with long, flat wooden sticks,

the lemonade she made
and gave to me to take to them
in the white enamel pitcher rimmed with blue,

the ropes of piss they pissed into the paint . . .
"Did not!"
"Did too!" I told my sister.
"They said it makes the paint *adhere*."

"Those two!" Mother laughed when we told her,
and she blushed and made more lemonade.
We'd never seen her so happy, joking with them,

her arm flung over her face for shade.
And by sunset the house was yellow too,
our wooden cave sealed thick and tight and safe
with paint and piss and lemonade.

Epithalamion

Dad, you think you can get rid of me?
No, I'm still running after you
on that half-gimpy leg that worried Mother so,
or sitting at your bus stop, or scolding you
for mowing down that baby cherry tree.
You think you can get rid of me?

No! What about the time
we were varnishing the bed frame
and I spilled some on the ground
and quick covered it with sand
and you smiled and looked away?
Okay? And the way your leather jacket

smelled of leather and warm you
when I hung it in the back hall after work?
You brought me graph paper from there
—the tiny squares! the tiny squares!—
and taught me how to whistle nonchalantly
when I was four.

By then we were already married,
you and I. Yes we were,
because once in your bedroom
you stood me on the bureau so I could see
myself in that tippy mirror
and put lipstick on me and Mother's veiled hat.

I knew we shouldn't do it;
I'd never been so afraid
of her in my life.
But you took my hand, led me to the kitchen
and announced: "Here is my new little wife,
Aurelia, here is my new little wife!"

The Petals of the Tulips

The petals of the tulips
just before they open,

when they're pulling
the last dark purple energy through the stem,

are covered with a whitish veil,
a caul.

I like them best then:

they're me the month before I was born,

the month Mother spent
flat on her back in the hospital.

The way I found out—

once, in round eight of one of our fights
I hissed at her, "I didn't ask to be born!"

and she threw back her head and howled,
remembering,

"You? You?

Hot as it was that summer
I had to lie there for weeks
hanging on to you.

You? You were begging to be born!"

The Monster's Flowered Apron

Not when she was unjust,
not when she hit me with a stick of kindling wood
until she drove a splinter underneath her nail
and bled,

not when she sent me up to bed
where I crouched creating monsters,

not even when she crept up later
wearing the monster's dress,
the monster's flowered apron,
and begged me to forgive her,

no, it was under the slow, blind caress
of her huge hands that desolation came:
something had mauled her so badly
it was only a matter of time.

The Ride Home

Maybe the ride home will never end.
The old Chevy purrs
and Daddy, quiet as usual,
just drives, not starting anything

and the tip of Mother's cigarette,
tiny Vesuvius, glows in the dark.

She smokes carefully because
the baby's sleeping in her lap and because
it might ignite the puffy gray fur collar
of the coat she bought when she was single
and had money of her own.

It smells like some animal when it gets wet
and from the back seat where I huddle,
the only pup awake,
it stands out against onrushing headlights
like a wolf's ruff in the moon.

All These Things She Kept in Her Heart

the knives she hid when her dad came home drunk

the time he lurched into her room
wearing her dead mother's flowered robe

the mattress-factory job she had
where that man said, "Let's go on a picnic, Hon,
I'll bring the wiener if you'll bring the bun"

her best friend snaring Daddy
and telling her, when she found out,
"Don't put me on a pedestal"

All these things she kept in her heart for years

and told them one by one
to me on Saturdays
when I was almost grown

and we cleaned the house together
because we did it best

always starting in mid-sentence

14

"yes, the priest,
he made my mother have that baby to the end,
even though he knew they both were doomed"

as if replying to a question

as if I'd dared to ask

her attention always fiercely on
the table she was waxing
or the window she was washing

the shriek of old sheeting against wet glass.

His Broad Clear Brow in Sunlight Glowed

What was done to her the year her mother died
and she was keeping house and coming home from school
with Tennyson beating in her head, her heart . . .
"And round about the prow they read,
The Lady of Shalott . . ."

What was done to her was dropped in conversation
by my father just last year: "Her old man,
she told me once, brought some friends home
and they were drunk and he, I guess, asked her,
you know . . . But she never told me any more."

The windows in our house were jewels.
How we polished them and dug ice diamonds
from the corners every week on hands and knees.
Once in a rage to clean under the piano,
she hoisted it alone and foundered like a stag.

He was *verboten*, but he was there
in the heavy, tin-lined, snap-back flour bin
she feared each time she used it. He got in her fists too
and made her smash my dreamy sister in the face
for forgetting to bring in the wash.

Dying, he sent for her from Michigan,
but she was canning beans that day
and didn't go, so he became the one jar
she was sure hadn't sealed, so she threw the whole batch
—seventy jars of squeaky crammed emeralds—away.

The Slaughter of the Innocents

"... Little did the clumsy customs official know that he was pawing through the luggage of the Lone Wolf, a man who had searched an entire house in the dark for an object the size of a pea—and found it!"

—Recollection from
The Lone Wolf, one of our books

What was he looking for? a pearl?
and did he find it in the button drawer
of the old, foot-pedal Singer?

Up to the wrist,
he lets three pounds of buttons
slide through his fluttering fingertips,

finds what he was looking for,
turns to go . . .
Lone Wolf, wait!

See the silver scissors gleaming there?
That summer Mother found out
she was pregnant once more

she grabbed them and hacked
her sweaty gray hair
straight off across the back.

No more church, no store.
She just prowled from stove to wash machine
to line

in that one square-necked, dark gray, home-made cotton dress
she wore
and wore,

stood ironing for hours at a stretch,
then made us look at, made us touch
the veins on the back of her leg,

hot black baroque slugs of blood.
Lone Wolf, try the house next door.
There are no jewels hidden here.

Lone Wolf, you still there? Listen then.
After three days of labor,
the baby finally came

and the first time I saw him
—she was in the rocking chair
surrounded by the others, nursing him—

I burst into tears.
She hadn't strangled him!
Bethlehem.

My Mother Trying to Die

When that clot hit her lungs, Dad said,
she snorted like a bull and wet herself
and shuddered to a stop right there beside him
in their bed
                but the Rescue Squad
strapped her to a board and broke three ribs
slamming her heart back to beating.

Then we arrived and gave them permission
to cut her throat
                to bring her bottled breath.

Death after death she died that week,
a warm corpse strung between the heart machine,
the lung machine.

                Her thick legs flung wide,
her green eyes shut tight,
she lay like a Klondike mail-order bride
trying hard to believe what he was saying:

It will be all right, lass. It will be all right.

The Week You Were Dying

Mother, the week you were dying,
we finished the bread you had baked,
the last of you at last inside me,

then every doilie, every chair,
every stick of furniture,
every inch of every rug,
the green one from the living room
where you were walked all night by Dad
the time you gobbled aspirin.

I stole relics: soap you'd started,
lipstick, half a piece of gum,
your red fishing shirt from Penney's
I still have on.

Ironing, I had to bend down,
so low had you set the board
for your long arms that grabbed the wheel
and tried to wrench us off the road
when Dad was going eighty through Nebraska.

Then, at the next motel,
calmly unpacking, handing the socks around,
you pretended, Kali,
that you hadn't tried to kill us all.

O Mother My Giant Redwood

The night before we flew your body home air freight
I dreamed your rage at finding you were dead
sent your coffin lurching down the aisle

dooming our plane in a crackling storm,

as if in death you could command
the force you feared each time, each time,

a thunderstorm.

I remember you wringing your hands,

moaning in the wind,
shuddering under strange stresses
those of us huddled at your base could only guess.

O Mother my giant redwood,

felled at last
you let us live.

You lay all morning quiet in the hold

nimbus   black bloodclots
dissolving   slowly letting go.

The Back Hall Was All Wrong

The back hall was all wrong,
the wallpaper sideways,

like bandages, like those rags
the Russian soldiers used to wrap around their legs.

Then I saw the lightswitch was papered over
—I could still smell the paste—

and the kitchen and dining room windows
and it was dark.

I started upstairs
but the upstairs was boarded and papered too,

a spongy pink lid
so close to my head

I had to lie down
with my arms at my sides and wait

and I was frightened, Mother,
and I was you.

Evening and Mother and I

Evening and Mother and I
were watering her roses

when a muddy animal,
part pig, part flabby, hairless dog

—ugly, ugly,
but with such sad eyes—

rose from the grass
and lurched toward her clean wash,

her warm, fresh-smelling dresses
on the line.

"Don't let it touch the wash!"
she shrieked,

but how could I stop it
who had never been able to stop it

when I was awake
and she was alive.

Something Silver in the Air

and then
a stab of joy:

corduroy whipping between my legs
as I walk

in the distance a flock of sparrows
flowing from tree to roof
and back again

and crouching in the grass that peasant,
that tulip leaf outlined in red

holding her little one
in thick, green arms.

II

We must represent men
either as better than in real life,
or as worse,
or as they are.

Aristotle, from *Poetics*

Delos

Knee-deep in grass and flowers
on that island where nobody dies

I thought of the death the gods are giving
to my first friend, that gray-eyed Polish Greek
named Delos, Delos, the boy who lived upstairs,
the boy with the rooster-peck scar on his cheek.

I didn't know he was an island.
He taught me to swear
but I sneaked out better food
and we fought the whole World War in our backyard.

The frozen garden furrows were the Burma Road
and when they thawed, Corregidor.

Our sisters were Tokyo Rose and her maid
pretending to play house,
but we took down every word,
then slipped away to break the code.

We parachuted from the airplane tree
behind Jap lines a thousand times
and cut ten thousand yellow throats.

If we were caught
the washpole was our torture stake;
the insects drove us mad.

Oh, Delos, last I heard
your sight was so dim, the tumor so advanced,

you set your house on fire with a blowtorch
by mistake, your four kids inside.

They put it out, of course.

O, dead-beat buddy,
slim commando slumped on your knees in the dusk
dragging on a cigarette swiped from your dad,

remember when I had to shake you?
Get up! Come in the house. We won the war.

Crackerjack

That kid in the blue sailor suit saluting
could be me, risen at last above the gang,
recruited, promoted, about to be packed off
to help Nimitz mop up the Pacific.
The prize was never much, some doll dish made of tin,
but the box gleamed, a neat, sharp-cornered brick
I dreamed of building with.
But I never had enough.
Too few peanuts too, and never the prize
I always half-expected deep within:
that Tom Thumb, tomboy sailor girl, my twin.

She Explained Worms to Me

Then one day the girl who lived upstairs from us,
whose mother had been hitched up as a horse
to plow her grandpa's fields up north
when she was young, took me under the porch
to our secret hiding place and there
she explained worms to me, and rats, and mice
and those gray slugs from under logs, mosquitos,
gnats, all stinging things, according to their preacher
as being sent by God to ha-ha bug us
lest we think that earth was Paradise.

Mr. Forstner

Because Molly was a hunting dog
whose pups came at the wrong time,

Mr. Forstner wouldn't let her keep them.
He pulled them from her pen,

blind and squirming
beagle pups.

We were kids
watching from the weeds

how he reached back,
grabbed one by the hind leg,

smashed it sidearm
against the stone foundation of the house,

tossed it to the right and then reached back
into the pool of live pups for another

and another—nine times,
and I've done it only twice.

Instead You Call

When you call, your cheerfulness thick as armadillo hide,
I'm supposed to help you keep it up.

You say I have no small talk. Well, you're right.
I don't care what color your new drapes are.

I want to know what you've done with her,
the girl who was you.

Remember that hard book you helped me write, our childhood?
The night our parents begged us to take sides?

The time our race to the toilet ended a dead heat
and we sat together laughing on the seat?

You scotch-taped your wedding pictures, but the rips still show,
ugly as a set of stretch marks.

Christ! If only you would barnstorm out of there.
Instead you call, circling like a wounded jet

through your spiral of topics—safe, banal—
your private holding pattern over hell.

The Strawberry Man

The strawberry man was too big for his wife,
I heard Mother tell a neighbor woman
that time he brought us berries by the case,
his nose a half a pint of berries
lumped up on his face. So they were divorced.

Plenty of men were bigger than their wives.
But what did too big mean?

Did it explain his whisky-broken voice,
his shock of uncombed salt-and-pepper hair,
the wary red-rimmed slits that were his eyes?

"She was such a little bit of a thing,"
my mother said. "Can you imagine the pain?"

The Orphans' Harmonica Band

Rosie, who else but you, back from the dead,
who told me that after having two kids
you spent most of every morning for a year
talking yourself out of killing yourself,

who else but you,
finding a drowned sparrow
at the bottom of the horse trough,
feeling those slick tin sides,
would ever after float a block of wood
upon the water as a raft?

New girl in town,
orphan living in a foster home,
you went sledding on your belly,
pretending to scorn our sleds.

Then, in sixth grade you got so horse crazy
you made a mane of your hair, hooves of your hands,
who else but you, who with your brothers,
scattered now and middle-aged,
once formed the wild, Italian nucleus
of the Orphans' Harmonica Band.

Andrew Van Wyck

He didn't fit the high school chairs;
his knuckles dangled on the floor.
He'd twist, get bored,
say anything he wanted to the teacher,
grownup to grownup; once he asked her,
"Are those still your same old teeth you've got there?"
In class he bit his fingers till they bled.

Blue eyes, quick grin,
hair like a field of wheat knocked down by rain.

Once after school he told me
how many cows his father had
and how his older brothers' farms were strewn
across the county, all on one party line,
so when his mother died his pa went to the phone
and cranked it, and waited, and told them all at once,
"Ma's dead."

Prayer after Mass

"Hail holy queen,
mother of mercy,
our life, our sweetness and our hope,

to thee do we cry, poor banished children of Eve,
to thee do we send up our sighs,
mourning and weeping in this vale of tears . . ."

But I didn't know that vale meant valley

and each time
I imagined the mother of Jesus
wearing a veil of tears,

her tears mostly,
but mine too because I had hurt her sweet son.

When she moved
the tears moved with her,
so she had to walk slowly

completely surrounded
by a shining bell of mist

and rainbows
and inside
about six inches behind the veil

not knowing why
she had to suffer so

she was.

Penelope

Of course she is tricking the suitors

unravelling by night
what she's woven by day

flirting at work
but trying to stay out of the bars.

After all, she's the wife of a sailor
and they've made a pact:

she never asks
and he never tells her.

Yet somehow she knows when his ship's in a port.

Those are the nights she stares at herself
and smokes

and breaks the spines of paperbacks
and tosses in that complicated bed

he made for them.

But this time it's been so long
and the pattern's so simple

that one day in spite of her stalling she's done.

Then teasing she shows the shroud to Amphinomus

and right on the dance floor
with everyone watching

he pulls her beneath it
and his prick is a tent pole

and she falls asleep dreaming

she's weaving
a wine-colored membrane,

that she's taut as a sail
for her bridegroom Odysseus again.

No Sigh of Jonathan

"But when they got back to the pool,
there was a hole in the ice
and there was no sigh of Jonathan."

Jared, that misspelling and the trust in your eyes
when you handed in your family history—
tragedy, as every family's is
in the retelling, each family reeling,
just recovered or about to be struck down:
the prosperous grandmother's swimming pool,
the ice, the brother running all the way home,
as they always do, to Mother—made me decide
to have you read them to each other.

"My great-grandfather was sitting praying
when General Denikin's men broke in
and threshed their swords straight through him."

Scott was right. Russia's Jews are only grain.
Oh Jared, weep no more for Jonathan.
We are all from the same place, same soft ice,
from, as Cheryl wrote, "the village of Pogrom."
We fled, but even here we're still black bread,
the sweet loaf on the lip of the pool. What's in it?"

Remember how we laughed when Molly read:
"The beach was so lovely that if I could,
I'd spend my entire life there in a minute."

Heroes

Those who do what must be done, over and over,
Joe Potowki's red-haired immigrant grandfather:
"He polished rubber combs in Trenton
six days a week, twelve hours a day,
rubbing the combs to a burnished glow,
and every Sunday after Mass
played his harmonicas for us."

And those who in sorrow have begun,
like Elijah Tilley, fisherman,
to learn to plant and cook and knit and wait,
as he did by the sea for his next glimpse of her,
"poor dear," who sailed before her bold Ulysses
into death, adventurous Penelope.

And the one I've loved since I was ten,
the old man in *Heidi* who hardly spoke,
but gave her bread and cheese and milk
and a clean, coarse sheet and let her climb
up the pegs to the loft. He knew
she would find mounds of loose, shining hay,
a perfectly round window and the moon.

III

Music i' the air.
  Under the earth.

Antony and Cleopatra 4.3

Wedding Night

The train was almost deserted,
so the wispy conductor decided
to tell us the story of his life.
"You kids just married?" Yes, we said.
"Hope you have better luck than I did.
After twenty years, my wife just split.
Took the car and left me the pickup
and my guts got shook to hamburger driving it."

You nodded solemnly and squeezed my hand,
your guts still firm and eager
and bright my wedding band.

The Method

Stanislavski, Vakhtangov, Pudovkin,
slapped awake by your passion for movies,
for acting, and bundled into your sleigh
—straw, stars, the horses' breath a cloud of steam—
I careered through the streets of your dream.
After love, we listened to all eight sides
of Boris Godunov. What courage it must take,
I said, to pour out your heart on stage.
You frowned, beetling your handsome brow.
You were in Strindberg's *A Dream Play* now,
learning your part, a coalheaver in hell,
by studying the Bronx Zoo gorilla's
slow-motion rage. Then you had to quit.
There was a baby coming, a living to get.

You've Got Your New Love

You've got your new love, I've got mine.
The house is cowering against the blow.
For Christmas, cold indifference.
We'll shop the January sales, we said.
We never did.
                  Then last night on the phone
you told me not to bother to come home in spring.
And the kids?
                  We're Jason and Medea now.
I'm sharpening my dagger
against your heart of stone.

The Hunt

That night keeps circling around me,
patient, waiting to close in:

Deliberately drunk,
I told him off.
Each word blazed forth, a torch
illuminating yet another turning.

Sweaty, inspired, shambling artist,
I stroked cave after cave
of black and ochre animals for him,
my animals, my sacred lust
that he could stalk but never satisfy.

"These last six weeks I've had more joy . . ."
I remember screaming.
Now come thick night and tell me,
what else did I say?

It's Dead

"Dad," he said. "It's Dad."
But I heard "dead" and I was right.
He was calling to report that you were dead.
And my first thought—I can tell it to you—
was that I was ruined.

For how could I write about your death?
And how could I write about anything else?

O churl! Remember our Shakespeare course?
How we laughed at the slaughter
in *Titus Andronicus*. We were so young.
Now we're frozen onstage in a play of our own:
you being beaten to death, I looking on.

What the Glacier Brought

What the glacier brought was a young man,
perfectly preserved after all those years.
Megève police pushed back the crowd
and hacked him out, axes flashing in the sun,
before his morgue, enormous tongue, moved on.
Then someone remembered the widow,
middle-aged now, growing stout and scrubbing floors
in the little wooden village down below.
They summoned her and watched her weep and pray.

Breathless they bring me the news and search my face.
But I am a terrible widow.
I can't pray. I left the village long ago.
And when I weep it's for us both, roped
together, inching across adulterate snow.

IV

Breathe your last free breath,
Because this—is love.

Anna Akhmatova, from *White Flock*

The Girl with Goat Feet

The girl with goat feet,
the girl with goat feet,
you were the girl with goat feet.

Straight out of that old Croatian legend
you came to my door and I let you in

gave you a bowl of milk,
a glass of gin

fell in love with you and then,
warming yourself by the fire,
"Look, I have goat feet," you grinned.

Painting after Vuillard

The woman on the left was added.

Bewildered,
she needs both hands
to keep her soupy purple robe
from falling open,

one of them precisely on her bush
or where her bush would be.

Instead,
an underpainted rug glows through
and everything below the waist
is flowers, flowers.

The one in burnt sienna staring out the window
is fine boned, moody and very much *chez elle*;
she knows the concierge and all the rents.

Plants, the blue and purple lamp globe,
lace, the brass legs of the clock,

French doors,
that rime of sunlight on your hair,
all down your side . . .

Now, from my blurred mouth,
bursts the first
of a million tender obscenities.

It's When I Tried to Tame You

Didn't the passengers of the Titanic,
strolling on deck, name the icebergs?

Make pets of them?

So I sat beside you at that party
consoling you, poor thing,

and woke up two days later,
two thousand miles away,

burning, sinking, burning.

News

I stumbled on that chunk of knowledge,
the fact that you are coming here again,
like a wild animal finding salt.

I tested it and then tore in:
deprived, deprived, deprived.

"Your body is your friend," you told me once,
watching my hands shake.

Outside my door two icicles
fused hip to hip and shoulder to shoulder,

slender arms outflung,

hang by the heels from the roof,
two crystal sides of beef.

Obsession

My body wants only one thing now,
your skin against its lips.

Night after night it stares in the dark

aching, inconsolable,
its throat a cage of tears.

And see where it haunts the parapet

begging for deliverance,
threatening to jump?

Well let it. People don't die from this.

To the Victor

"I want you both," you whispered on the phone.
Dazzled, emboldened, ignoring the word both,
I swaggered across the continent
to claim you for my own, found you morose,
evasive. We could never be alone,
unless—then you thought of the wooden horse.

"Make her fall in love with you too," you said.
Yes. Then hypnotized she'd seize the rope
attached to this strange gift and pull it through
the gate and I'd leap out and slaughter her
unless she saw me first. "I want you both . . ." Dead?
It's dark inside these sweating walls of fir.

Icon

Miles from any place I'd ever been before,
I clung to you,

the air cool green,
the ivory of your skin,

the way your eyes darted
when I touched you.

Like startled birds they were,

and your grave smile
forgave me my only sin:

that it had taken me so long to find you
and place you in the sacred corner,

The *krasnie ugol* of my hut,
to the left as you enter the door.

O Voie Lactée,
O Corps Blancs des Amoureux . . .

O Milky Way, O the white bodies of lovers . . .
At last I understand Apollinaire.

You're here, asleep beneath my hand,
lips parted, so far from me, so unaware.

O voie lactée, o corps blancs des amoureux . . .
You stir, say something in your sleep

and now we're stars.

Chinese Baby

Chinese baby screamed all night,
Chinese baby skinned alive
it sounded like.

Two is company, three's a crowd.
White flesh my food, white sheet my shroud,
summoned here but not allowed,

I'm jammed between the wall and thee
I dare not touch lest she should see.

Wind from the airshaft fussing
with the wind chimes in the hall,

swelling beast between my legs
not fussy at all.

I Dreamed That Dream

I dreamed that dream
of finding heart-shaped, fist-sized stones
as red as rubies all along the path
when I was half mad with longing for you
who had somebody else and wanted us both
and told me it would be all right,
you would make her understand.

It was a mountain path in Italy,
the sun on gray shale,
and every few steps
I bent down with such joy
to pick up a new heart,
each one more perfectly formed than the last,
more full of light.

The Role of the Beloved

"The role of the beloved,"
I wrote before it started,
"is simply to be loved:
to be plucked from the crowd,
brought back to the studio,
taught how to hold a pose
without sweating or trembling,
then stared at until she dissolves,
flesh become cloud . . ."

I wrote, hoping to skip a step,
hoping to transform
desire directly into art
by equating myself with that painter
who hired girls from the village
to pose for her naked
and using their blushes,
created those glorious clouds.

But it didn't work.
The fathers of the girls complained.

And I had to spend a whole year in hell,
in apartments, in stations, in phone booths,
waiting for the beloved to call,
for the stalled blood to move in my veins.
For I had to learn
that the role of the beloved
is to do whatever she god damn pleases,
to be a Tamerlaine, to grind,
if she chooses, ten thousand skulls
beneath the wheels of her chariot,
or one skull ten thousand times.

Recitative

You dared touch me
when you weren't free
to let me love
the only way I can,

au fond?

If only this were an opera,
someone stabbed in a sack and dumped.

If only people like me
were still possible,
I could say

"You dared touch me?
Well then let me die
by those same sweet, helpless hands."

Put me out of my misery.

And Your Favorite Had Her Face Kissed Raw

Back to that first dream I had of you:
you were kissing a whole procession of women,
not just me,

and your favorite had her face kissed raw.

Next time I come to earth
I'll build my churches small as Greek chapels:
low doorways to repulse the charges
of the horses of the Turks.

The dream ended with the three of us
on a dirty blanket.

Somebody's going to get hurt.

Versailles

The upper floors of the palace are honeycombed
with boudoirs just large enough to hold the bed,
the vanity of a woman once desired,
taken as mistress for awhile, then cast aside.
Forbidden and by then too proud to go home
—they had known le Roi Soleil—banished from his sight,
all night, all day they prowled the rustling corridors
the rest of their lives, perfecting their French, their spite.

I'm telling you this so you will understand why I,
listening to you dismiss me, could only stare
at your hands winding, unwinding a yellow cord
you'd found somewhere, why I couldn't raise my head
for one last astonished look into that
shimmering blue hall of mirrors, your wretched eyes.

Zouave

What did I do before I met you?
Who hurt me then?

I should have known
from your Zouave eyes,
those spoked suns that never lied

—whose pupils, four strokes
of Vincent's pen
form a tiny clenched spider
of terrible truth—

that you would make me leave you
when you were done.

Things to Do Today:

not think of you,

avoid oranges
because of the delightful way
you attacked and devoured them,

shun anyone
with dark hair, white skin,
wild eyes,

avoid high ceilings,
finches, plants, all city sounds,
not think of you,

admit that I'm

the show-off I read about
who dangled a mouse above his mouth
and swallowed it by mistake,

and had his insides torn to pieces
by a suffocating creature
trying to escape.

V

She loved poetry, books, trees, the sky,
and her own thoughts.

Konstantin Paustovsky,
from *The Story of a Life*

Indulgence and Accidents

". . . These 7 years were full of indulgence and accidents. A doughnut or two a day wasn't unusual and I demolished a 57 Chevy, which was just the beginning of a horrible driving record. Adding to the trouble my brother Guy drove over me with the Massey-Ferguson. Didn't hurt me much and all in all the years went very well."

—from Aura's autobiography

then marriage, the baby
and making him so mad
in that N.Y. apartment

he threw the phone
and broke the wall
but I got up

at dawn to write
so he did too
and woke the baby

then Greece, and baby #2
and my breasts got hard as stone
and so the midwife milked me

as gently as she could
staring out the window
dreamy eyed

and talking to the other women in the room
for such a long sweet time
I went to sleep

and woke up in Connecticut
with something wrong with me,
the need to tell the truth

and be a perfect human being
so I started writing poetry
my brother Guy

"Is the poem so transparent
that it will reveal my failings?"
is my first official entry

*Didn't hurt me much
and all in all
the years went very well*

until my brother turned
and saw I was still moving
and swung the Massey-Ferguson around

Come Closer if You Want to Know

Someone is circling around me,
peering over the edge.

It's been so long

but still I know
exactly when to flex my glistening surface

when to subside.

I can be silent for hundreds of miles,
but what am I thinking?

Come closer if you want to know.

But know too that when they asked me
if there was anything I wouldn't write about

I had to say no.

...dîn

We were sitting in a circle
on an undulating porch of woven reeds

studying a poem
about a golden insect
or a bird.

Thick black letters danced on the page

and all that remained
when I awoke
was this shining fragment   . . . dîn

and my need to say:

"He finished reading.
He was exhausted.
My hand was resting lightly on his thigh."

The Children of

The children of deaf parents cry
without making a sound.
They make unhappy faces

when they are unhappy.
But what if their mother does not turn around?
What if she rushes off blindly to a place

where she will be tortured
by the exquisite obsession
of her choice,

wake up weeping in Central Park,
on the wrong bus in Queens,
or standing in an inch of gray ice

in a phone booth in the Village,
paralyzed by the indifference
in the beloved's voice

yet noting the exact nuance
for the poem, the real obsession,
that cauterizing curse.

Palabras Para Hoy

My sense of time is shot.
Everything that ever happened
is right here on top of me,
screaming to be fondled,
fed and put away.

My glasses are too strong.
They won't let my eyes
slide out of focus
until I get completely smashed
and stamp on them

and flush them down the toilet
as Uncle Armin in the nuthouse did
with every pair they gave him.

Last year all year I spent
muttering my poems to myself,
applying them like poultices
until I sucked them dry.

That's what we do, you know:

like Highlanders fanning the sick
with pages of the Bible,
we fan ourselves with words

and still we burn
and still we burn.

To Muriel Rukeyser

I saw you only twice,
once leaning on a friend and a cane,
head high, your wide-open face,
your splayed, caped body moving
like a great ship in the rain

unashamed of anything
that body ever did or could do,

then at that reading,
your last poems larger than life,
huge on the page
because that's the way you had to write them
so you could see.

Yet you watched over your city
to the end.

Now let us watch with you
and take you by the hand
and walk with you
past all those tender, cardboard poems
propped in shop windows:

"Any Kind Sandwich"
"Every Monday Closed, Rose."

February 11, 1963

Everything she touched that day
was rough   or smooth
then very rough   or very smooth.

She kissed her stucco babies
with lips as slick as worms
and then she set them down.

And men? Ah, men were coarse as tripe.
They filled the map!
What was it she had read?

The tubing in one testicle, unfurled,
would stretch the length of England,
from Land's End to John O'Groat's.

And Spain, oh Spain where once they lolled
was now a puke-pink rock
so far below

she knew her clunky feet
would never land her there
even as she knelt

and thrust herself
into that oven filled with hissing, pissy gas,
his plan for her, his urinal.

Getting Ready to Translate Akhmatova

—for E. L. and W. L.

White house, gray shiny-painted porch
hugging the hill

the woman on her tractor cutting hay
right down to the woods

right down to the one birch
bending its white neck . . .

It's a cliché!
I'm even cleaning mushrooms.

Upstairs in the guest-room mirror,
grass of Parnassus

—creamy petals lined with green—
floats like Easter vestments

stiffly Orthodox
and doomed.

Muse, sister, I know you're here:
túcha is stormcloud, néba, sky

and this morning Wassily set an extra place
at the table

without knowing why.

Amimetobian

For they made an order betwene them, which they called Amimetobian (as
much as to say, no life comparable and matcheable with it) one feasting ech
other by turnes, and in cost, exceeding all measure and reason.
      —from Plutarch's *Life of Marcus Antonius*

Exiled to Voronezh
for the poem he wrote about Stalin
(". . . His fingers are fat grubs . . . His cockroach whiskers leer . . .")

driven to paranoia
and that leap from the hospital window
that dislocated his shoulder and cleared his mind

recalled and kept revolving, kept on "Hold"
in the hundred-kilometer zone,
that wheel of wooden villages surrounding Moscow

arrested again
and sent to a camp
where he died of "heart failure"

Osip Emilievich Mandelstam
had. nothing in this life

except his poetry:
"Today is all beak
and no feathers . . ."

a wife who went with him,
memorized every word he wrote
and brought it back from the dead

and the friendship
of Anna Akhmatova,
his peer.

But wasn't that everything?

Seated on the shabby couch
they nicknamed "the Bessarabian carriage"
they rode all night

flinging each other lines from Dante,
from Pushkin,
from their own new poems

getting high on Ariosto,
on *chai iz stakana*, tea from a glass
and slang remembered from their student days.

They were—and they must have known it—
the Antony and Cleopatra
of that wolfish season

". . . one feasting ech other by turnes,
and in cost,
exceeding all measure and reason."

Akhmatova

She called her poems swallows and they were.
For fifteen years of mornings they took flight,
recklessly cleaving and cleansing the air,
skimming Tver's impassive fields of wheat,
the ponds and giant parks of Tsarskoye Selo,
swooping with Petersburg's fine, slanting snow
to delineate cruel, tender lovers
"As no woman has ever been able to do."

Then Gumilev was executed, Blok died,
and never again were her words unweighed.
She was Cleopatra, her son confined,
a northern Cassandra vilified.
Stalin called her his nun. Banned, spied on,
flown from the siege to Tashkent in bloom,
she was thawed, refrozen, toyed with, permitted
to outlive Osip, Marina, Boris, everyone.

To My Next Poem

Maybe we'll meet
like that old Russian couple in the lobby

kissing full on the mouth
at ten in the morning.

Or are you already here?

sailing down that complicated coast of Norway,
the sutures of my skull,

Brahma's handwriting
—the legend says—
upon the head of man.